Russia

St Petersburg

Stephen and Scharlie Platt

www.leveretpublishing.com

Russia: St Petersburg
First published - October 2017
Published by
Leveret Publishing
56 Covent Garden, Cambridge, CB1 2HR, UK

Vases in the Hermitage Museum

ISBN 978-1-912460-12-0

Russia
St Petersburg

Steve and Scharlie at Peterhof

Russia 2009

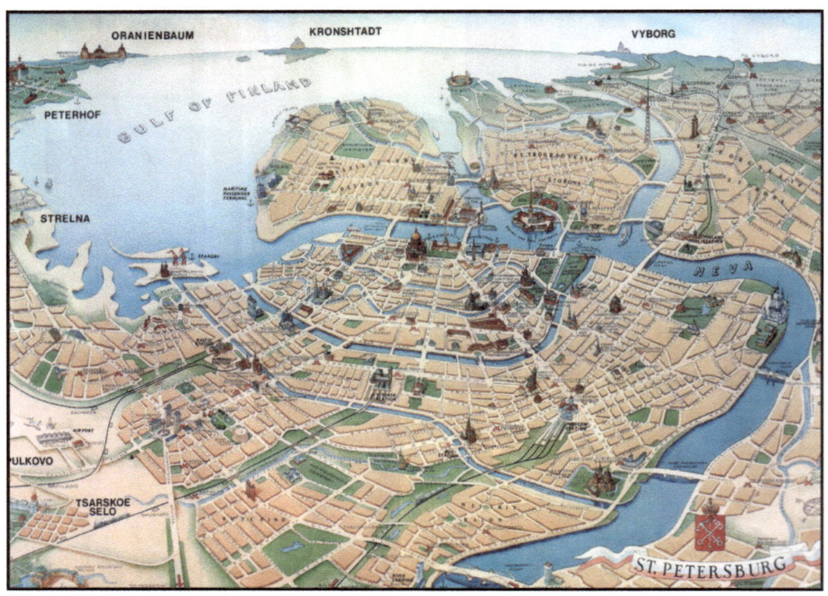

Map of St Petersburg with our hotel almost in centre of the map

St Petersburg

Sunday 24 May

Wadim met us at St Petersburg airport. It's a typical small ex military airport and there is a long queue for passport control. The escalator from the arrivals halls descends into the queues so there is an almighty mix up. There are lots of people, both men and women, in wide brimmed Russian army caps with hammer and sickle on a red star. Everyone is friendly and, despite the crush, very good humoured.

We have come to Russia to attend an EU research project meeting. The project is called ISAAC and is about promoting heritage tourism. As well as specialists in communication there are tourism managers from Amsterdam, Genoa and Leipzig, the cities we are focusing on in the project. Our hosts are from the State Russian Museum In St Petersburg and we are meeting in one of their buildings, the Mikhaylovskiy Zamok (temple).

We are staying in a fabulous hotel next to the Fontanka River near

Some of the EU ISAAC project team

Dostoyevsky Square and in walking distance of Nevsky Prospect, the main shopping street. From our table at breakfast we can see a black dog. It looks like a mongrel and is following an old woman. It stands on its hind legs begging and she stops and feeds it bread from her plastic shopping bag. The woman crosses the road towards us when the lights change but the dog stays with the people waiting to cross the other junction. As soon as it sees them move it runs forward and crosses the road safely and sets off down the street at right angles to us searching in each doorway for food.

The market opens early and is winding down by the time we get there just after breakfast. There are stalls piled high with produce – fresh fish, vegetables, fruit, honey combs dripping with sweetness and stone counters slick with soft cheese and bowls of curd. The abundance tempts you to a splurge of consumption but overwhelmed by the choice we just wander along the aisles drinking in the sights and smells.

The Vladimir Church is in Dostoyevsky Square near where we're staying and we go in during a service. It seems very friendly, but Scharlie, Wadim and Jing are nervous about intruding. The service in the nave of the church is being

Looking towards Church of Our Saviour of the Spilled Blood

Kuznechnyy rynok (market)

Vladimir Church in Dostoyevsky Square

conducted by two or three bearded priests in green and gold vestments and tall white hats. The congregation seem to be locals that have popped in from surrounding homes or businesses. It all seems homey and working class. The church has only recently been renovated and restored for church services and was used as an ambulance station till 1990. There are separate services

Nevsky Prospect

going on in the two transepts. I saunter over and the others hold back but people are very welcoming. It's as if this is all new and they are proud that foreigners have come in to see their worship. A young priest with a black beard is giving a sermon surrounded by his congregation, who are all standing. A young woman in a skimpy white shift leans back against one of the stone pillars, her face enraptured by the service. It all seems fresh and close to Christ's ministry in the Bible.

The city centre is not at all what we expected. Nevsky Prospekt is thronged with beautiful girls walking arm in arm, smiling or laughing, or attentively hanging on the arms of Armani clad older men. Most are dressed to the nines in skimpy chic fashion and improbably high heels. They are slim and tanned, not at all the dumpy babushkas we were expecting.

The Hermitage Museum is magnificent. It's huge and a little daunting. But we are given a tour by a marvellous guide who has been laid on by our hosts in the Russian Museum. He runs us through some of the main galleries and gives us the confidence to return on our own. Scharlie goes back when I'm in a meeting and I go back on the morning we're leaving. The rooms are almost

Inside the Hermitage

empty and the custodians quite relaxed about you going up to the art to have a closer look or to take a photograph. We focus on the Impressionists – there are lots of Manet, Chagall and Gaugin. The collection is impressive and the many paintings owe much to the private collections of Seigei Shchukin and Ivan Morozov, who recognised the originality and quality of the new French art and began collecting in 1898. Shchukin commissioned Matisse to paint the two paintings, *Dance* and *Music.* We go down to the classical galleries and find the Roman exhibits rather boring although it's interesting examining the faces of famous Romans. The Egyptian gallery is more interesting.

We also have a guided tour of the Russian Museum, which is housed in the Mikhailovsky Palace where our meeting is being held, and are taken in chronological order through the great Russian art, from the icon painters through to the early revolutionary artists who were suppressed by Stalin. We've heard of Repin and recognise his painting of Barge-haulers on the Volga,

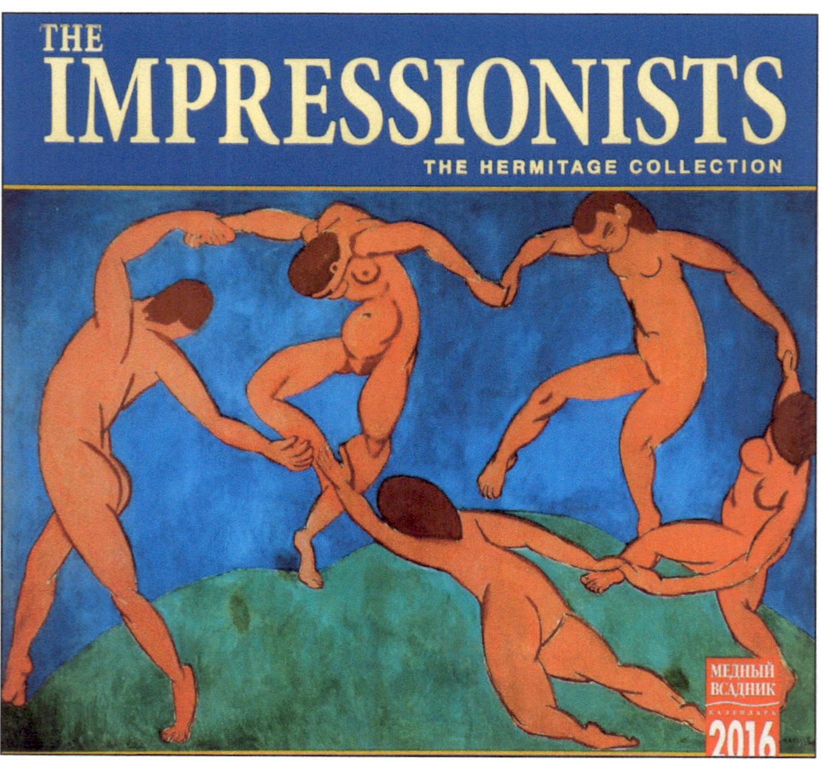

We are thrilled by the Impressionists in the Hermitage

but know none of the others. Again our guide is marvellous and explains the context of the works he focuses on. We are particularly taken by an icon of the Angel with the Golden Hair and later, in the Hermitage, buy a facsimile. We are intrigued by a surprisingly matronly painting of Catherine the Great promenading with her dog in the Tsarskoe Selo park; and note the Last days of Pompeii by Karl Bryullov, the Wave by Ivan Aivazovsky and the Ceremonial

Angel with the Golden Hair

Meeting of the State Council by Repin with its hundreds of miniature portraits.

But the thing that most impresses us is the Church of the Spilled Blood,

Catherine the Great in the Russian Museum

built on the site where Emperor Alexander II was fatally wounded by political nihilists in March 1881. Similar to St Basil's Cathedral in Red Square in Moscow, it is one of the most striking sights in St Petersburg.

The square behind the Hermitage, the Winter Palace, is Dvortsovaya Ploshad. It's huge and we cross it a number of times during our stay. There are soldiers with the traditional wide brimmed visor caps. It's the time of the White Nights when it never gets really dark and one evening we go for a boat trip around the city with some of the ISAAC people including Ian, Antonio and Frank. Antonio is in a lovely mood, hugging Frank and joking with everyone and trying to persuade the boat captain to let him steer. We set off from the River Fontanka which encloses the old heart of the city, past the Summer Palace and out into the Neva and finally cross the river and sail behind the Peter and Paul Fortress. We walk across the bridge between the Winter palace and the Admiralty that crosses the Neva to the Strelka and Vasilevskiy Island and wander along past palaces and mansions that are now largely military museums or academies.

We see a notice outside a concert hall on Nevsky Prospekt for a piano

Boat trip on River Fontanka with research assistants Wadim and Jing

recital later in the day. The hall is the Glinka, or small, Philharmonic Concert Hall. The woman in the box office was kind and talked to the manager, a woman, who said yes there were seats still available near the front. We have lunch and arrive at the theatre when it's thronging with people. I present the tickets but am stopped by a rather officious lady who, I think, is explaining that we only have one ticket. I tell her I definitely paid for two and try to reach into the bin into which she has thrown my ticket stubs. She gets very agitated and calls over a guard. I realise this is getting out of hand so just put my arm through Scharlie's and march in. We are seated in aisle seats near the front when the officious ticket collector turns up with a imperious looking tall women who also speaks a little English. We hold our ground and she eventually leaves us to it as the concert is about to start. I reach into my pocket and find the missing ticket and go after her to apologise!

The pianist comes onto the stage to enthusiastic support. She is a dark haired middle-aged beauty with a generous bosom She's very good and obviously well known in Russia. She has a lot of elderly admirers in the audience, many of whom present her with bouquets at the end of the recital.

Piano recital in the Glinka, or small, Philharmonic Concert, Nevsky Prospect

We ride the metro with Wadim and Jing. The underground stations are modelled on those in Moscow and have the same impressive art nouveau architecture with lots of marble, mosaic and elegant lighting. Known as people's palaces they were built in the 30's during the reign of Stalin. They have the same wide gauge as the main railway lines. The platforms are separated from the tracks by doors that only open as the train arrives and are supposed to hold back flood water. It is illegal to take photographs on the metro so we don't take out the camera, even though we'd like to and Wadim risks a quick shot with his camera. I sit next to a plump woman who is immersed in a small format magazine rather like a Reader's Digest. Looking over her shoulder I can see it is about cooking and she goes through each page carefully reading each recipe and then either ticking or crossing the title. They all seem to be variations of dumpling stew.

We have a day off and visit Peterhof with Wadim and Jing, the palace modelled on Versailles by Peter the Great. It's a warm sunny day and we go to the Grand Cascade first with the Sampson fountain and the surprise water features that spray the Japanese tourists and make them shriek. We walk all

Jing and Steve and the fountains of Peterhof

The Peterhof Palace

Children playing in the fountains at Peterhof

round the estate and decide not to bother with the palace itself. It's been renovated recently and all the domes and fountains are covered in gold leaf that glitters in the sun. It looks incredibly gaudy. We rest on benches near the waterfront and watch the hydrofoil ferries scooting back and forth. We decide to return by sea and the ride is much more pleasant than the mini-bus we took on the way there.

We return to the hotel and pack. It the end of our brief trip to this cultural capital. The airport bus is old and ramshackled and people toss their rouble notes on a carpet spread over the engine cover next to the driver when they get off and he doles out the change while driving. Luckily we find somewhere to perch with all our bags.

Dinner on our last night

We learn how to use the CAR camera

Peter the Great

Peter the Great and St Petersburg

Peter the Great, founder of St Petersburg, ruled the Russian Tsardom and later the Russian Empire from 1672-1725. 'The Great' because Peter expanded the empire into a major European power and led a cultural revolution that modernised Russia and had a lasting impact. Standing at 6 ft 8, Peter was literally head and shoulders above his contemporaries both in Russia and throughout Europe.

Peter implemented sweeping reforms aimed at modernizing Russia and he reorganized the Russian army along modern lines and dreamed of making Russia a maritime power. To improve his nation's position on the seas, Peter sought to gain more maritime outlets. His only outlet at the time was the White Sea at Arkhangelsk and he needed a better seaport since Arkhangelsk was closed to shipping for months during the winter.

The Baltic Sea was at the time was controlled by Sweden in the north, while the Black Sea and the Caspian Sea were controlled by the Ottoman Empire and Safavid Empire in the south. While attempting to create an Ottoman Alliance to help gain control of the Black Sea while visiting the Netherlands, Peter studied shipbuilding in Zaandam and Amsterdam.

Peter made a temporary peace with the Ottoman Empire and turned his attention to maritime supremacy in the Baltic and declared war on Sweden. It was in this period that he founded St Petersburg, situated on the Neva River, at the head of the Gulf of Finland on the Baltic Sea. In 1703, during the Great Northern War, Peter the Great captured Nyenskans the Swedish fortress at the mouth of the Neva River and soon he began building the Peter and Paul Fortress, which became the first brick and stone building of the new city.

St Petersburg was built by conscripted peasants from all over Russia and tens of thousands of serfs died building the city. Peter moved the capital from Moscow to Saint Petersburg in 1712. The Commission of Stone Buildings of Moscow and Saint Petersburg ruled that no structure in the city could be higher than the Winter Palace and during the reign of Catherine the Great in the 1760s–1780s, the banks of the Neva were lined with granite embankments.

On November 7 1917 the Bolsheviks, led by Vladimir Lenin, stormed the Winter Palace in an event known after as the October Revolution, which led to the end of the post-Tsarist provisional government, the transfer of all political power to the Soviets, and the rise of the Communist Party.

Interior Vladimir Church in Dostoyevsky Square

Inside the Hermitage Museum

Fyodor Dostoevsky 1821-1881

EU ISAAC project team

EU ISAAC meeting

'Barge-haulers on the Volga' State Russian Museum, Ilya Repin

'Ceremonial Meeting of the State Council,' State Russian Museum, Ilya Repin

'Steve admiring The Wave' by Ivan Aivazovsky

'The Wave' State Russian Museum, Ivan Aivazovsky

Peterhof Palace

The Peterhof Palace is a series of palaces and gardens laid out on the orders of Peter the Great on a bluff 25 km to the west of St Petersburg where the water of the Baltic was deep enough for ocean going vessels. This was Peter's Summer Palace that he would use on his way coming and going from Europe through the harbour and island fortress at Kronstadt.

Grand Palace at Peterhof

Grand Cascade at Peterhof

Wadim and Jing, research assistants from Nottingham University and Grand Palace

The Hermitage at Peterhof

Monplaisir Garden at Peterhof

Marly Palace kitchen at Peterhof

Garden at Peterhof in front of Marly Palace

Lion sculpture at Peterhof

Pier at Peterhof, Scharlie waiting for the hydrofoil ferry back to town.

Illicit photo on St Petersburg metro

Escalator in the metro

St Petersburg Metro, 'The People's Palace' (opened 1955)

www.ingramcontent.com/pod-product-compliance
Lightning Source LLC
LaVergne TN
LVHW052302100826
845147LV00001B/121

* 9 7 8 1 9 1 2 4 6 0 1 2 0 *